Author: Allison Lower
Picture Researcher: Bridget Tily

First published in Great Britain in 2005 by
FREDERICK WARNE & CO.
Published by the Penguin Group,
Penguin Books Ltd, 80 Strand, London, WC2R 0RL, England
Penguin Books Australia Ltd, 250 Camberwell Road,
Camberwell, Victoria 3124, Australia
Penguin Books Canada Ltd, Alcorn Avenue, Suite 300,
Toronto, Ontario M4V 3B2,
India, New Zealand, South Africa

2 4 6 8 10 9 7 5 3 1

ISBN 072325754X.

Printed in Italy

Contents

Welcome to Wisteria Lane

Behind the pristine white voile curtains lies a hidden world of secrets and lies.

There's a bit of desperate housewife in all of us. This guide will show you how to turn yourself into your favourite housewife in a few easy steps.

So let's meet the residents of Wisteria Lane.

The Mayers
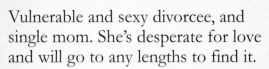
Susan Mayer

Vulnerable and sexy divorcee, and single mom. She's desperate for love and will go to any lengths to find it.

Julie Mayer

The oldest 13-year-old on the block. Streetwise teen who acts more like a mom than her mother.

Mike Delfino

A sexy plumber with a dark and deadly secret that makes him even more irresistible to all the woman in the lane.

The Scavos
Lynette Scavo

Career woman turned serial mother. She's found that being a full-time mom is harder than any job she's ever had.

Tom Scavo

Loving husband and father who is blissfully unaware of the fact that his wife is slowly being driven mad by her out-of-control children.

Porter, Preston, Parker and Baby Scavo

The most terrible twins, their just-as-naughty older brother and the baby – children you wouldn't wish on your worst enemy.

An UNOFFICIAL Guide To Being A Desperate Housewife

THE VAN DE KAMPS
Bree Van De Kamp

21st century Stepford wife. Everything has to be just so; her children, her house and, most importantly, herself.

Rex Van De Kamp

A respectable, middle-class husband with a secret penchant for whips and nipple-clamps.

Danielle Van De Kamp

A model teen on the brink of sexual discovery – she hopes.

Andrew Van De Kamp

Proven hit-and-run driver and a homosexual-in-waiting.

THE SOLIS'

Gabrielle Solis

The vamp of the street with a taste for young gardeners.

Carlos Solis

Latino lothario and crooked businessman.

THE HUBERS

Martha Huber and Felicia Tilman

Local dead busy-body and her blackmailing sister.

EDIE BRITT

The tramp of the street and proud of it. Presently homeless.

THE YOUNGS
Paul Young

Widower and father with a terrible secret which led to his wife committing suicide.

Zach Young

As troubled a child as you can find. He thinks he killed his little sister, Dana, but there's so much more to his story.

Mary Alice Young

Shot herself after being blackmailed about her past, but still very much a part of life on Wisteria Lane.

Sex and Shopping

When your friends are your neighbours, there's nothing easier, or nicer, than meeting to catch up on all the gossip. The ladies of Wisteria Lane find plenty of fun ways to fill their days that you could try too.

Let's Do Lunch

The venue should dictate the outfit. If it's a breezy al fresco restaurant, then tailor your look accordingly. Either a strappy summer dress or slim-fit trousers and heels will suit. Don't forget your designer handbag, a must for ladies who lunch.

Be prepared to put aside a few hours. These things shouldn't be rushed. A lovely bottle of chilled, crisp white wine is de rigeur. What better way to spend a day than telling your friends your juiciest secrets — just as long as you know they won't breathe a word to anyone.

Charity Events

It's important to be seen at the right events. There will be a host of charity fundraisers that you should become involved in, particularly anything to do with children or saving the planet. These are a great place for networking and generally catching up on all the latest news.

Shopping

There's nothing more fun than spending the day at the mall with friends — particularly when you have your husband's credit card in your handbag. But apart from putting aside time for lunch — this will be a quick salad as opposed to the type mentioned previously — you should plan your trip with military precision. There should be a hit list of all the top designer shops you need to visit. We recommend those who really look after their clientele — friends can sup champagne while you try on outfits. It can be a real giggle when you go for the more risqué looks. Underwear shopping can be enormous fun too — a trip to *Agent Provocateur* is a must for any woman who wants to keep her husband (or lover) under her thumb.

Dangerous Liaisons

If you do have a lover — and why wouldn't you — the girls can help out there too. If you arrange a rendezvous, ask a trusted confidante to cover for you in case your husband ever rings and can't get hold of you. If your lover has a reason to visit you at home then all the better but, if not, pick a quiet motel — it doesn't have to be five star, just clean and discreet — at least five miles from where you live, to lessen the chances of detection.

An Unofficial Guide To Being A Desperate Housewife

How To Chill Out The Bree In Your Life

We've all got a friend like Bree – she's cool and sophisticated, but incredibly uptight. Here are a few ways to help her loosen up.

1. Take her for a massage – it will do her good to have a strange man's hands rubbing her body.

2. Hide all her cosmetic products to liberate her from the need to look perfect. You may have to endure being told off when you're found out.

3. Take her on a charity parachute or bungee jump – she'll realise how good it feels to hear herself scream.

4. Have a girls' night out. Fill her full of tequila and get her dancing to a bit of 1970s disco.

5. Take her shopping. Clothes maketh the woman, but the twinsets and pearls that maketh this woman are DULL. Try and introduce a bit of silk or satin into her wardrobe.

6. Buy her some naughty underwear – it might just get her in the mood for a bit of passion, plus it'll give her poor henpecked husband a night to remember.

7. Take her on a girly holiday. It's amazing what a bit of sun, sea and… salsa dancing will do.

8. Video her going about her everyday, uptight things. When you play it to her she might be horrified to see herself as others see her and realise just how boring she really is.

9. Arrange a girly night at your house. Make the strongest cocktails you can and get her drunk. It'll loosen her tongue and she'll feel much better if she shares some of the secrets she carries around like a millstone, like her bedroom activities.

10. If all else fails – get her indulging in a flirtatious extra-marital affair. Adoration should loosen her up and put a spring in her step. Just keep her away from pistol heirlooms.

How To Spot and Befriend A Bitch

With neighbours like Edie about, it's imperative you learn how to survive living with a bitch. It's best to keep on her good side, so read how to spot her and then make her your friend – it's the safest option...

Spotting A Bitch

1. She'll be cool, confident and oh, so two-faced. She'll probably be showing a lot of flesh, even if she's just popping to the shops.

2. She'll fight you to the death for any available man on the block.

3. By means fair or foul, she'll try to make you her confidante – blackmail is usually a firm favourite of the bitch.

4. She trades in her men more often than you change your knickers.

5. She'll flirt outrageously with your husband/boyfriend/son.

6. She may well compliment you on your outfit – but only if hers is sexier, and she'll always do it in a patronising tone.

7. Her boyfriends will always be in the highest tax bracket and she'll have the presents to prove it.

8. If there's a busybody in the street, you can bet your bottom dollar she'll be her bosom buddy.

BEFRIENDING A BITCH

1. Smile sweetly and agree with everything she says, even though you know she'll be gossiping about you behind your back.

2. Get in there quick! If he's hunky and he's new, stake your claim.

3. Do not, under any circumstances, tell her your secrets. She'll be crafty and try to gain your trust in order to get you to spill. But don't fall for it and don't ever get drunk with her.

4. Make sure you know who her latest flame is, you don't want to date him by accident. She'll eat you alive.

5. Don't ever leave her alone with any of your men. Keep your husband close and your son closer.

6. Smile graciously, nod and move away. You know it's not sincere but, hey, it's better than her telling you how huge your backside is.

7. If at all possible, pick a plumber to date, unless of course he happens to be an incredibly hot plumber with a deep, dark secret, then you're just asking for a fight.

8. There's no doubt that she'll be plotting and scheming behind those net curtains. Grit your teeth and smile innocently.

LADIES' POKER NIGHTS

If there's one thing that all the ladies of Wisteria Lane share,
it's a love of poker. So why not host a girlie game yourself?
Just pour a few cocktails for your players (see the fab cards at the back),
read the rules and get ready to bet a slice of your housekeeping on
poker's fastest and meanest seven-card game – Texas Hold'em.

THE AIM OF THE GAME

The aim of the game is to make the
best five-card hand that you can, using
both the two cards that each player
is dealt face down, and the five
community cards dealt face up in
the middle of the table. Every hand,
one player will get the dealer button
(a small disk marked with a D).

THE DEALER BUTTON

The position of the dealer is
important, as the two players to the
dealer's left are required to place
their bets blind (i.e. without seeing
the hand they are dealt). This is
known as "posting the blinds".
The dealer button moves to the left
after each hand, so everyone acts as
the dealer and everyone is required
to "post the blinds".

BLINDS

The player to the immediate left of the dealer posts the small blind, and the player to the left of that player posts the big blind. The blinds are placed in the pot to start the betting and give players an incentive to enter the hand. They also mean that the winner of the hand can never walk away completely empty-handed.

The size of the blinds are dictated by the stakes that you're playing at. The small blind is typically half the minimum bet of the game, while the big blind is typically the same as the game's minimum. For example, if you're playing at a £10 minimum bet and £20 maximum bet table, the small blind will be £5 and the big blind £10.

THE OPENING DEAL

Once the blinds have been posted, moving clockwise round the table from the dealer, each player receives two cards dealt face down that only they get to see. These are called "pocket cards" or "hole cards".

It's now time to start betting.

BETTING FOLLOWING THE OPENING DEAL

At this stage, each player is betting on whatever hand they feel their pocket cards could lead to. The betting starts with the player to the immediate left of the big blind.

For this round of betting, each player has three choices: to fold, raise, or call (i.e. match) the big blind. As the players who posted the blinds have effectively opened the betting, each player has to at least call this bet to stay in the hand.

PLAYING POKER: THE RULES

WHO'S THE DADDY?

The betting goes round the table in a clockwise direction until each player has either called, folded or raised. If no-one has raised by the time the betting returns to the person who posted the big blind, this player may check their own blind, fold or raise. To "check" means to decline to bet further at this stage.

The first round of betting is at the lower level of stakes, so in a £10 minimum bet and £20 maximum bet game all raises are increments of £10. For any round of betting there can be an opening bet and no more than three raises. So, after the third raise, betting is said to be "capped" and there can be no more bets.

THE FLOP

Now it's time to use "the flop". The flop is the set of three cards that are dealt face up in the middle of the table. Each player can use these community cards to construct their hand. They're dealt in the middle of the table and known as "the board".

Now it's time for another round of betting, again at the lower level of the stakes. This time, the betting starts with the player to the immediate left of the dealer, regardless of whether the dealer is still active in the hand or not. The player to the left of the dealer will keep the initial action for the rest of the hand. Apart from that, the betting process is the same as pre-flop betting.

THE TURN CARD

Once betting has finished, another card is dealt face up on the board. This is called the "turn card", and again can be used by all players to build their hand. The betting after the turn is now at the higher level of the stakes, so in a £10 minimum bet game and £20 maximum bet game, all bets will now be increments of £20.

THE RIVER

It's time for the fifth final community card to be dealt called "the river". Now all five cards have been dealt, each player can see what their best five-card hand is. Now comes the final round of betting, again at the higher level of the stakes. eg, £20.

THE SHOWDOWN

Each player who's still in the hand shows their cards, starting with the last person to bet. The winner is decided by the rankings shown next. If a player wins a pot by default because every other player has folded then there's no showdown. The winning player can decide whether to show their cards.

WINNING HANDS

The following hands are shown from the lowest ranking through to the highest.

HIGH CARD

The highest ranked card is an Ace. Ranking runs from the Ace down through the cards to 2.

Pair Any

Two cards of the same rank, for example two Queens. The ranking of pairs mirrors that of the descent of numbers through the cards, so the strongest pair is a pair of Aces and the weakest is a pair of 2s.

Two Pair

Two sets of two cards of the same rank, for example two queens and two 6s.

Three of a Kind

Also called "trips". This is where you have three cards of the same rank, for example three 7s.

Straight

Five cards in sequential rank order. For example Queen, Jack, 10, 9, 8. An Ace may be used as both a high and a low card.

Flush

Five cards of the same suit, for example five diamonds.

Full House

A combination of a pair and three of a kind.

Four of a Kind

Four cards of the same rank, for example four Queens.

Straight Flush

A straight (see bottom of previous column) but with all the cards in the same suit.

Royal Flush

The Daddy of all poker hands! A royal flush is a straight flush involving the Ace, King, Queen, Jack and 10.

TRUE LOVE SECOND TIME AROUND

If, like Susan, you're divorced and looking for love again, then here are some simple dos and don'ts for finding the man of your dreams.

Do...

* Take care of yourself. It's tempting to gorge yourself on chocolates and ice-cream, but this only leads to feeling fat and wanting to hide in comfy clothes. Then the men asking you out will look more Russell Grant than Russell Crowe.

* Be natural. But if you haven't got that cute, vulnerable, girl-next-door thing going on, fake it. Men like nothing more than a woman who needs protecting.

* Be coy. By your age he knows you've got a past, but if he thinks you've been round the block too many times, then he won't want to take you for a test drive.

* Be honest, but only within reason. If your husband left you because your domesticity bored him, tell your new man that he got sick of your love of literature and cordon bleu recipe experiments.

* Get out there. You won't meet a man by staying in. Hit the town at least once a week with your girlfriends. Go to bars you know are packed with single men. If you haven't got someone to go with, take up a hobby and make new friends.

* Don't take second best. Your ideal man needs more than just his own teeth and hair. You should go weak at the knees and miss him every second you're not together. You deserve the real deal.

An Unofficial Guide To Being A Desperate Housewife

Don't...

* Accept your singledom. It's easy to give up after a failed marriage. There are plenty more gorgeous, available men out there and you deserve one of them.

* Mention your 13-year-old daughter on the first date. Firstly, because he'll think you won't be able to do anything spontaneously, and secondly, because he'll realise just how old you really are.

* Steal your daughter's boyfriend. You may feel incredibly young at heart, but dating a 16-year-old really is out of the question. It doesn't matter how cute he is.

* Hang out with beautiful friends. Try to ensure that you're as good looking, if not better looking, than the girls you're on the pull with. It's just sound business sense.

* Sleep with him on the first date. Make sure he comes back for more. Do you really want your future husband thinking you're an easy lay?

* Date a friend's ex. No good can come of it. She is bound to be unhappy and you really don't want him comparing you to her in bed.

* Get locked out of the house naked. It doesn't look great if you're caught hiding naked in the shrubbery. Not only will guys think you're an incredible klutz, but it's also not a flattering light for them to see your naked body in. Always aim for candlelight for that first unveiling.

Getting Away With It

(Gabrielle's Guide to Getting it on and Not Getting Caught)

When your totty's as young and fit as John the gardener, you have to be prepared to go to any lengths to keep your affair a secret. Gabrielle has ten top tips to show you how to get away with it.

1. Close to Home

When you need some lovin', it's handy to have your lover only a short drive away, and even better if he happens to be just outside your front door pruning your hedges, all hot and sweaty… Short of a gardener, consider your plumber, mechanic, window-cleaner or builder.

2. Huntress

Make sure you have him hooked before going in for the kill. The last thing you want is for him to turn you down and go running to tell your husband. Be sure he's taken the bait and is eager for the catch.

3. Informed Infidelity

You should take into account…

a) His marital status. He shouldn't be married, it's hard enough to keep a secret from one spouse, let alone two.

b) His age. The younger, the better. He'll be eager and willing (to please and to learn), and he'll always be able to rise to the occasion.

4. RELIABLE STAFF MEMBER

Definitely the best option as there are many reasons for him to be in your house should your husband arrive home unexpectedly. You can tell your hubby that your lover was just helping you change the lightbulb on that exceedingly high chandelier.

5. POST-COITAL

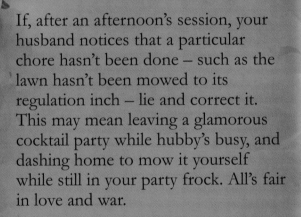

If, after an afternoon's session, your husband notices that a particular chore hasn't been done – such as the lawn hasn't been mowed to its regulation inch – lie and correct it. This may mean leaving a glamorous cocktail party while hubby's busy, and dashing home to mow it yourself while still in your party frock. All's fair in love and war.

6. SNAKE EYES

If you have a nosy mother-in-law who's coming between you and your man, then use any ammunition you have against her. It's handy if she has an addiction such as gambling. Just drop her off at the nearest casino. She'll be out of your hair for hours.

If this doesn't work, then take her to a mall, cram her bag full of tagged goods and watch as she gets arrested for shoplifting.

7. NEIGHBOURHOOD WATCH

There's a chance that someone might catch you at it. If you're careful, it should be no one more important than a local kid. The promise of a brand new bicycle with all the trimmings should buy the little darling's silence. Even if it's the local busybody who discovers your activities, the same rule applies (although you'll have to up the gift value). Never be afraid to bribe.

8. PUPPET MASTER

Get the rest of the help on-side (see bribery ideas above). Then they can lie for you if you're running behind schedule to meet hubby or caught in the house with your lover.

9. DIRTY HABIT

Tell your husband that you've developed a slight case of OCD. This can then be used to explain your constant showering so you don't reek of loverboy's scent.

10. AND FINALLY...

Ensure you have the best sex EVER with your toyboy. There's no point risking your show home for someone that doesn't do the job.

EDIE'S ENCOUNTERS

(GETTING FROM FIRST TO FOURTH BASE IN FORTY SECONDS)

There's no denying that Edie's the neighbourhood tart. If you want to be as successful with the boys as she is, then bite the bullet (unless you can find something more enticing to pop in your mouth), dress in your sluttiest little number and head on down to the local pick-up-joint.

Ask him how he has his eggs in the morning as you promptly lead him from the bar or, for those of you feeling really adventurous, forget that dull ride home and drag him into the ladies for a quickie. Exceedingly satisfying and a lot less bother than trying to get rid of him the next day.

He will, by now, be by your side, so moisten those lips and slip him the tongue – keep it slow and sensual to make him wonder what else you can do with that tongue.

Enjoy!

Make and maintain eye contact while performing a sex act on your bottle of beer. N.B. If you haven't already seen it, we strongly recommend you rent a copy of *In Bed With Madonna*.

Identify your prey – the more handsome and dumb-looking the better.

10 SECONDS	20 SECONDS	30 SECONDS	40 SECONDS
PICK HIM	BEWITCH HIM	LICK HIM	HAVE HIM

HAIR

We highly recommend long flowing locks for that vixen look and, as Edie knows, there is no such thing as too much peroxide. Always wear it down and NEVER be afraid to flick it – the more you throw your head back and laugh sexily, the better. But if you're follicly challenged, then make sure it's either tousled or spiky (depending on length) for that just-got-out-of-bed look.

NAILS

Long, Long, Long! If they look like they'll take half the skin off his back, you know you're on the right track. Also, if possible, paint them pillar-box red.

UNDERWEAR

A sparkly G-string is essential. If you're wearing trousers, they should be low slung enough for the G to peek over the top, or if you're wearing a skirt, a Sharon Stone moment would also work well.

WAX

Nobody loves a yeti. When he hits fourth base he's going to want to see skin – and lots of it. If your lady garden looks like a brillo pad, or God forbid a bird's nest, then get yourself down the beauty salon sharpish. This is probably the only time you need to think like a girl guide and be prepared.

MAKE OUT LIKE MAISY

(MAISY GIBBONS' GUIDE TO RUNNING A BUSINESS FROM HOME)

Working from home is a delight for any housewife – it keeps you active without the bore of having to travel to an office.

Here are a few top tips to ensure your business goes with a bang.

SELLING YOURSELF

Marketing is key to any thriving business, but it's best done with class and discretion. A quiet word in the ear of a prospective client, at the right function, is usually all it takes to swap business cards. Of course, word of mouth is very important too. So always make sure the client goes away happy and hopefully he will tell his rich friends.

OFFICE EQUIPMENT

Install a separate phone line – you don't want an unfortunate mix-up with one of your husband's work colleagues. Also, it would be terribly embarrassing if someone called to make a golf date with your husband, and thinking he's one of your regulars, you offered to polish his club.

Buy your own laptop – it's always best to keep business and pleasure apart and you really don't want any of the family stumbling across your working proposals.

TOOLS OF THE TRADE

It's important to keep yourself fit. You're a walking advertisement for your business, so flabby thighs and a wobbly bum are unacceptable. Spend at least an hour a day working-out and don't look at it as work – your husband will appreciate it too.

An Unofficial Guide To Being A Desperate Housewife

Discretion

Keep your client list small. When working from home you don't want hordes of strange men coming and going at all times of the day and night. Plus, even though you're at home, work is work and it can be very tiring. You'll need some downtime too.

Make sure you know your family's schedules. The last thing you need is for your husband to come home early and find you bent over the ottoman with a man in a gimp mask rogering you senseless. That really won't do.

Protect your contact book with your life. Your clients expect complete and utter privacy in regard to their business dealings. You don't want names falling into the wrong hands.

Any Other Business

Don't waste valuable time with the mundanities – employ a cleaning and laundry service as you will find that there's an awful lot of sheets and other sundries to wash. You will also be far too busy to worry about housework. Unless a client has a particular penchant for the feather duster.

Update your health and safety certificate regularly. A clean and healthy body (and home) is essential when working in any sort of business.

Important

Make sure the only handcuffs you're ever seen in are covered in red fluffy fur, not cold steel with a policeman attached to the end. Unless it's the Chief of Police making his monthly visit for a little light bondage.

TOUGH LOVE

(BREE'S ADVICE ON KEEPING YOUR HUSBAND HAPPY IN THE BEDROOM)

Although Bree may be the definition of prim and proper, she's had to learn to change her tastes to satisfy her bondage-loving husband. Find out how you too can turn from good girl to bad girl in the bedroom.

GOOD GIRL

1. Run a hot bath for your husband and fill it with aromatherapy oils.

2. Leave a trail of red rose petals from the front door all the way to the bedroom.

3. Fill the room with hundreds of pretty candles for a romantic atmosphere.

4. Buy a pretty negligée to remind him how you looked on your wedding night.

5. Feed him chocolate-covered strawberries dipped into champagne as a sensual treat.

6. If you're feeling very naughty, trail a silk scarf gently over his body.

7. Perform fellatio on him as a special treat on the last Sunday of the month.

8. Make love with the lights on to be risqué.

9. Whisper sweet nothings into his ear.

10. 'Hold each other' afterwards.

BAD GIRL

1. Cover him head to toe in talcum powder so he'll slide easily into his rubber bondage gear.

2. Buy a bunch of 24 long-stemmed roses (with the biggest thorns you can find) and thrash him about the back and buttock area.

3. Using a large church candle, pour hot wax onto his most sensitive areas. Nipples and crotch are firm favourites.

4. Less is more. Matching red leather peephole bra and crotchless panties rarely fail to miss the spot. A leather mask works well too.

5. Have a wide selection of food available to suit every whim. It could include whipped cream, chocolate sauce (hot or cold), syrup, cherries, ice-cream and porridge oats.

6. Tie him spread-eagled to the four corners of the bed and whip him senseless with a riding crop till he screams for mercy.

7. Whatever hubby wants, hubby gets. Whenever, wherever.

8. Blindfold him while he's still tied up and do unspeakable things to him over which he has no say or control.

9. Swear at him. The more vulgar the better. We know ladies don't use bad language, but this is the one time you've got to get down with the kids.

10. Stick on the hardest porn you can find (or tolerate), wait until your batteries are recharged, then get back on that pony. Yee hah!

Raising Hell

(Lynette Scarvo's Contented Baby Theory)

It's not easy being a mom to four little boys under the age of six, especially when three of them are the spawn of Satan. But Lynette's still hanging in there, so let's see how she manages to survive.

DAILY DOSE

Sometimes there's only one way to get yourself through the day – with medication. If your kids are half as hyperactive as Lynette's, then they've probably been prescribed ADHD medication. Count yourself lucky and get your hands on their *Ritalin*. You'll be able to go three days without a wink of sleep. However, if you find strangers backing away from you at bus stops, and shop assistants pressing their help buttons at the sight of you, maybe you should lessen the dosage.

PUNISHMENT

In this day and age, parents can get themselves into all kinds of trouble with corporal punishment. A tiny smack can be enough to get your darlings on the phone to Childline. So be sneaky and find a neighbour to do it for you. The Bree in your life will probably have no qualms about putting them over her knee and giving them the spanking of their lives. So if you're too squeamish to do it yourself – send them over to her house.

However, it's essential to get tough yourself at times or else the kids will walk all over you. Car journeys can become a real issue. You may find that stopping and leaving them by the side of the road is a good option. Only don't leave it too long to return to collect them – a well-meaning passerby may call social services and the next thing you know you'll be labelled a bad mother. Probably by someone who doesn't have children themselves. The cheek.

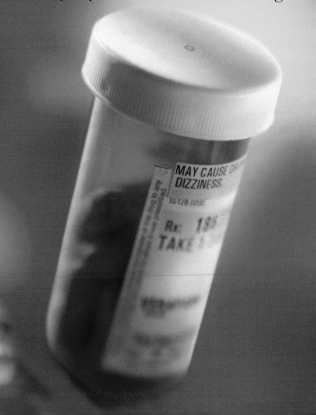

MAY CAUSE DR
DIZZINESS.

10128 00:00

Rx 18
TAKE

An Unofficial Guide To Being A Desperate Housewife

When Needs Must

A nanny is absolutely essential and she's got to be top notch. You can't have any old riff-raff bringing up your children, or no one will want to marry them and you'll be stuck with them forever. But make sure she's not too attractive. We all know men can't resist a pretty woman under their nose all day. Unless of course you're keen to get out of your marital duties, in which case make sure they're pretty but not too smart.

Interfering Neighbours

There's nothing worse than being criticised for letting your kids misbehave – especially when it's beyond your control. So keep a handy supply of food nearby to throw at meddling neighbours. Or, even better, persuade them to accompany you and the kids on a day-trip, then accidentally lose them while you nip off for a cappuccino. That'll open their eyes to the joys of motherhood.

Teach Him A Lesson

It's frustrating when your husband only sees the kids on their best behaviour. This can't continue. Cajole your hubby into a night's babysitting, then load the little angels up on the most sugary e-treats you can lay your hands on. They'll be bouncing off the walls all night. Now let's see how he likes it.

Be Tough

When it comes to getting your child into the best school – again, be prepared to do anything. It may be wise to medicate them before they see their new principal. Lie – yes of course, they're always this quiet and well-behaved.

GETTING YOUR MOM A DATE

JULIE MAYER'S TOP TIPS

It's not every daughter who wants their mom to find a new man, but Julie's not like every daughter.

She's more mature than Susan and she's prepared to help her mom find love any way she can. So here's how to find love the Julie Mayer way.

PLOT

The hardest part is finding suitable candidates, so don't be afraid to try out a variety of options.

* If you've got a hot teacher, then why not suggest some home tuition? Who knows, perhaps their eyes will meet over your geography atlas.

* You know the man in the pharmacy has been making eyes at your mom as she's collected her water-retention pills. Arrange for a home delivery.

* If he happens to be the cute neighbourhood plumber, then stick something down the plug hole to block it – a homework project is good.

* Likewise if he's an electrician. Fusing the lights works well – your mom will look better by candlelight when he pops round.

* Put her details onto an internet dating site. Okay, you may end up getting replies from lonely weirdos, but there must be some normal guys out there looking for love. Mustn't there…?

An Unofficial Guide To Being A Desperate Housewife

Prepare

If your mom's a bit out of practice, you may need to remind her how to get ready for a date.

* Tidy the house and make sure there are clean sheets on her bed – no one likes a slob.

* Take her shopping for something sexy to wear.

* If your mom's anything like Susan, then make sure they have their date at a restaurant. You cannot afford for him to taste her cooking.

* Buy her condoms. It's been so long since she last pulled a man that her pill will be at least three years out-of-date.

Execute

This is the hard bit – you're really going to have to pull out all the stops to ensure that everything goes to plan.

* Arrange to stay at your dad's for the night – nothing says passion killer like a teenage daughter in the next bedroom.

* If you can't go away and he's coming to dinner, then feign some (non-contagious) illness and lock yourself in your room, saying you'll be dead to the world and won't be able to hear a thing.

* Ensure there's no chance of any sexy female friends of hers showing up unannounced (particularly if they look and act like Edie Britt).

* Get her to act sexy. When he comes to the door to collect her, remind her to stick out her boobs and suck in her tum. In fact the mantra 'tits and ass,' should be foremost in her mind all night.

And if she doesn't pull after all that, then resign yourself to having her live with you for the next thirty years. Arrgghhhhh!!!

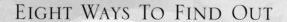

Is Your Son A Gay Joyrider?

Eight Ways To Find Out

Kids are clever at keeping secrets, so you have to be even cleverer to find out what they're up to. If you suspect your son's been at it with cars and boys, then here's an easy-to-follow checklist to find out for sure.

1. Ask him repeatedly to bring his girlfriend home to meet you. If he can't rustle one up, then get suspicious.

2. While watching re-runs of *Baywatch*, check out his reaction to slow motion running sequences of Pamela Anderson and Yasmine Bleethe. If he doesn't get a stiffy – like every other man on the planet – then be worried.

3. Frequently test him on his highway code knowledge and give him a driving consequences quiz with questions like:

If you accidentally mowed down a neighbour, would you:

A) Stop to see if she was alright and call an ambulance

B) Run to the nearest house and ask for help

C) Get back in your car and race off leaving her to die in the road.

(N.B. C IS THE WRONG ANSWER)

4. Buy a copy of a straight porn magazine and a gay porn magazine and leave them where he's likely to find them. If the straight one goes missing, breathe a sigh of relief (after checking your husband isn't locked in the bathroom with it), but if the gay one goes walkies, well…

5. Steal his mobile phone and check all his messages. This should definitely give you a clue as to which locker room he's peeking into at school.

6. Unblock the gay porn channel on *Sky*, then go out for the night. Return home earlier than expected to see if you catch him watching *Big Bendy Boys*.

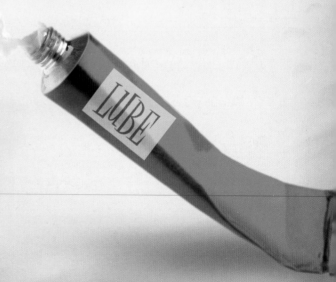

7. Ask him to invite his friends round for a pool party. Pretend to go out but secretly watch everything through binoculars at your bedroom window. If there's one place young boys with lustful intentions can't keep their hands off each other, it's in the pool.

8. If a hit-and-run accident does take place in your street, immediately (but quietly so as not to alert the neighbours) check his car for indentations and blood.

If any of these points apply to your son, then get him to the nearest shrink and driving school – in no particular order – as soon as possible.

Getting Ahead In The PTA

By Lynette And Bree

When your child attends the best school, it's important to be involved as much as possible. Here's the Lynette and Bree way of contributing to their children's school lives.

Lynette

1. If you get roped into making all the costumes for the school play, don't worry what they look like – just make sure you finish them by whatever means possible.

2. If you don't like the way the Head of the PTA goes about things, then stage a revolt. Get the other mothers on your side to oust her.

3. The only way to get your voice heard at school is to offer them a large cash donation. Not only will it benefit your children, but it will also give you incredible leverage should the school ever try to expel them.

4. The other women like to have coffee mornings to sit around gassing about how great their kids are. If you ever get roped into having one, then make sure it's so lousy that they never ask to have it at your house again.

Bree

1. Make sure you leave a clear window of at least four weeks to enable you to make the most spectacular costumes you can for the school play.

2. It's important that all the mothers band together. If everyone gets on, then it can only be a good thing for the children.

3. You should try to make a donation to the school fund whenever possible. Surely there can be nothing more satisfying than seeing a new school library built with your name on it.

4. The PTA coffee mornings are an institution. They should be planned and properly organised so everything is just so. Have all the china ready, with doilies on the plates. Bake a large selection of cakes so everybody will find something they like. These are mornings to look forward to.

An UNOFFICIAL Guide To Being A Desperate Housewife

LYNETTE

5. If you have to take part in Sports Days, at least put all your effort into winning the egg and spoon race. You'll show them who's boss.

6. Make your husband do some of the work and get him to offer some great work placements for the older kids. They have to out do all the other father's placements, so if he has to organise special trips away for them, then so be it.

7. They're always looking for fundraising ideas so why not suggest all the members of the PTA pose nude for a calendar just like the Women's Institute did.

8. Get involved in the end of year Prom. These are always such dry events and could do with some livening up. If you see someone spiking the punch – let them. It never did you any harm, did it?

BREE

5. School Sports Days are great social events. It's wonderful to see all the children enjoying themselves and it's lovely to take part in the races – as long as you don't get any overly competitive mothers.

6. Why don't you offer to take the children on day trips to exciting places of interest like the City Art Museum? They learn so much and always really appreciate it.

7. Fundraising for the school can be so much fun. You can plan bake sales and jamborees and maybe even a golf tournament.

8. When it comes to the Prom, you should help your son or daughter to be crowned King or Queen in any way you can. Take them shopping for the best outfits money can buy. Ask to be a chaperone on the night as we all know what the little monsters can get up to without the correct adult supervision on hand.

GABRIELLE'S BEAUTY BIBLE

We can't all be model material, but we can all make the best of ourselves with a little help from Wisteria Lane's answer to Selma Hayek.
Read and learn…

SEXY SEAFOOD SALAD

30g (1oz) butter
6 tbsp dry white wine
A handful of torn basil leaves
salt and pepper to taste
1 clove of garlic, crushed
125g (4oz) scallops
500g (1lb) fresh mussels
half red pepper - cored, seeded and sliced thinly
125g (4oz) cooked and peeled prawns
125g (4oz) cooked crab meat
half red chilli - cored, seeded and sliced thinly
1 tbsp chopped parsley
half quantity garlic dressing
6 black olives
6 anchovies

Melt the butter in a large pan and fry the scallops and garlic for five minutes. Add the wine, basil, salt and pepper and bring to the boil. Add the mussels, discarding any that have already opened. Cook over a high heat, shaking the pan for about five minutes until the shells have opened. Discard any that do not open. Drain and leave to rest for five minutes, then remove their shells. Mix together the scallops, mussels, crab, prawns, red pepper and chilli. Add the dressing and parsley and toss well. Arrange the olives and anchovies on the top. Suggest serving on a bed of rocket and mixed leaves, topping with parmesan shavings and a drizzle of balsamic vinegar.

To make the fabulous garlic dressing you'll need:
2 tbsp white wine vinegar,
5 tbsp virgin olive oil,
salt and pepper to taste,
2 crushed garlic cloves,
half a lemon.
Place all the ingredients in a screw top jar and shake well.

8.15 AM
Wake up. Have a detox drink of hot water with a dash of freshly squeezed lemon juice.

8.45 AM
An hour of intensive yoga. You have to suffer to be beautiful.

10.00 AM
Have a warm shower, switching to cold water thirty seconds before the end to tighten up any flabby bits.

11.10 AM
Go for a facial.

12.30 PM
Have sex with the gardener.

1.15 PM
Have lunch. See salad recipe.

An Unofficial Guide To Being A Desperate Housewife

2.00 PM
Have sex with the gardener.

2.50 PM
Go for a seaweed body wrap. Gets rid of a few unwanted pounds around the thighs.

4.25 PM
Go for a three mile run.

5.45 PM
Have sex with the gardener (if not too tired at this point).

6.45 PM
Have second shower before hubby comes home.

7.15 PM
Exfoliate before liberally applying moisturiser.

8.20 PM
Eat a delicious low calorie dinner with your husband. See chicken recipe.

9.45 PM
Attend social function. Only drink champagne – anything else overly dehydrates skin.

11.15 PM
Have a cleansing cup of herbal tea – green tea if possible – to flush out the day's toxins.

11.35 PM
And as a bit of a treat for him – have sex with your husband!

Yummy Mexican Chicken

2 tbsp vegetable oil
2 onions
2 garlic cloves
2 large tomatoes
1 green and 1 red pepper
2 green chillies
4 chicken breasts skinned and sliced into large strips
salt and pepper
300ml (half pint) of chicken stock
1 tsp chilli powder
2 tbsp white wine
1 tsp vinegar
75g (3oz) hard cheese such as Cheddar or Monteray Jack

Chop the tomatoes into cubes. Peel and chop the onions and puree with the garlic in a food processor. Cut the peppers and chillies in half and remove seeds. Cut the peppers into thick slices and the chillies into thin strips. Heat the oil in a large pan, add the chicken strips and fry over a high heat for five minutes until golden. Remove from the pan and season with the salt, pepper and chilli powder. Add the tomatoes, peppers, onion puree and chillies to the pan and pour in the chicken stock stirring continuously. Slowly bring to the boil, then add the wine and season with the vinegar and salt and pepper. Reduce to a low heat, place the chicken in the pan and simmer for 20 minutes. Grate the cheese coarsely and sprinkle over the top. Cover the pan with a lid, turn off the heat and leave for five minutes or until the cheese has melted. Suggest serving with brown rice and a crisp salad of cos lettuce sprinkled with pine nuts. And, to get your juices flowing, serve a shot of tequila as an aperitif!

How To Get That Body

By Susan Mayer

There's no denying that Susan Mayer has a body that most of us can only dream about. But here are her secrets on how she does it – intentionally and unintentionally.

1. Being of a nervous disposition is very handy. If you're always stressed and fretting you'll be surprised at how many calories you can burn off without even trying.

2. Why bother going to the gym, where you'll be judged by a bunch of lycra-clad fitness freaks, when you can pop in a yoga DVD and work-out at home? Half an hour each morning should do the trick. Remember not to do it naked though as it can be terribly embarrassing if a neighbour pops their head round the door to see if you're home.

3. Being a terrible cook really helps. If every meal you make tastes like charred porridge, it's amazing how quickly the weight drops off.

4. Having a neurotic mother is in your favour. Just as you're going to put that delicious chocolate fudge brownie in your mouth, you can hear her telling you that it will go straight to your hips. A marvellous appetite suppressant.

5. Suspecting any of your neighbours of foul play will keep you so busy you'll forget to eat. You'll also be so wrapped up in running around spying on them that you will get a great work-out for free.

6. A teenage daughter comes in incredibly handy. Not only will you want to prepare really healthy meals for her, but the desire to fit into her clothes will definitely keep you on the straight and narrow.

7. If, like Susan, you work from home, then you will often be asked to look after neighbours' children. There's nothing like a day spent running around after little tearaways to keep you fit and healthy.

8. Falling in love, or even just having a crush on a neighbour, can stop you wanting to eat at all. He's all you think about…

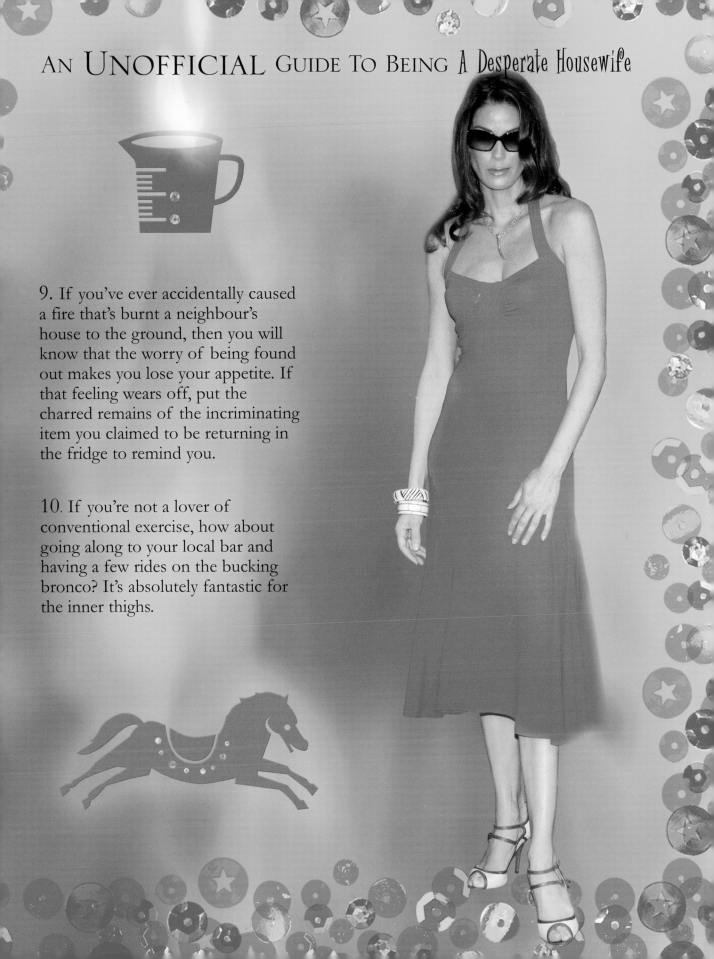

9. If you've ever accidentally caused a fire that's burnt a neighbour's house to the ground, then you will know that the worry of being found out makes you lose your appetite. If that feeling wears off, put the charred remains of the incriminating item you claimed to be returning in the fridge to remind you.

10. If you're not a lover of conventional exercise, how about going along to your local bar and having a few rides on the bucking bronco? It's absolutely fantastic for the inner thighs.

PERFECTLY TURNED OUT

There's no denying that Bree Van De Kamp is the best-groomed woman in Wisteria Lane and while you may not want to go for the full Stepford wife look, we could all do with a few tips on being better dressed.

HAIR

* The key word is sleek. Even if you have short hair, it should be glossy, shiny and styled to perfection.

* There's no such thing as too much hairspray if you want your hair to stay in place.

* If you're going to put it up, then a trip to the hairdressers is essential. Do not attempt to do it yourself as you will never be able to achieve that just-stepped-out-of-the-salon look which is imperative for an up-do.

* You should visit the hairdresser at least once a month for a trim and a colour. Split ends and black roots – or God forbid grey hairs – are simply out of the question.

* A selection of headscarves is essential. If you're doing the gardening or anything else energetic, then tie a pretty headscarf round your head to ensure your hair doesn't get messed up.

* Wash it every day. Dirty hair equals dirty morals.

MAKE-UP

* Under no circumstances leave the house without full make-up. Even if you're just popping out for a pint of milk, reapply first.

* Powder is your best friend. Ladies shouldn't perspire, so make sure you never have a shiny nose.

* Never use too much. You can't go wrong with browns, pinks and oranges. Remember, you want to look like a lady, not a lady of the night.

ACCESSORIES

* Accessories complete an outfit so have plenty to choose from. Keep them in labelled boxes according to colour, and day or evening wear.

* Have a few basic pieces that go with anything, just in case you have to leave the house in a hurry.

* Always, always make sure your handbag matches your shoes.

* Never mix silver and gold. Not ever.

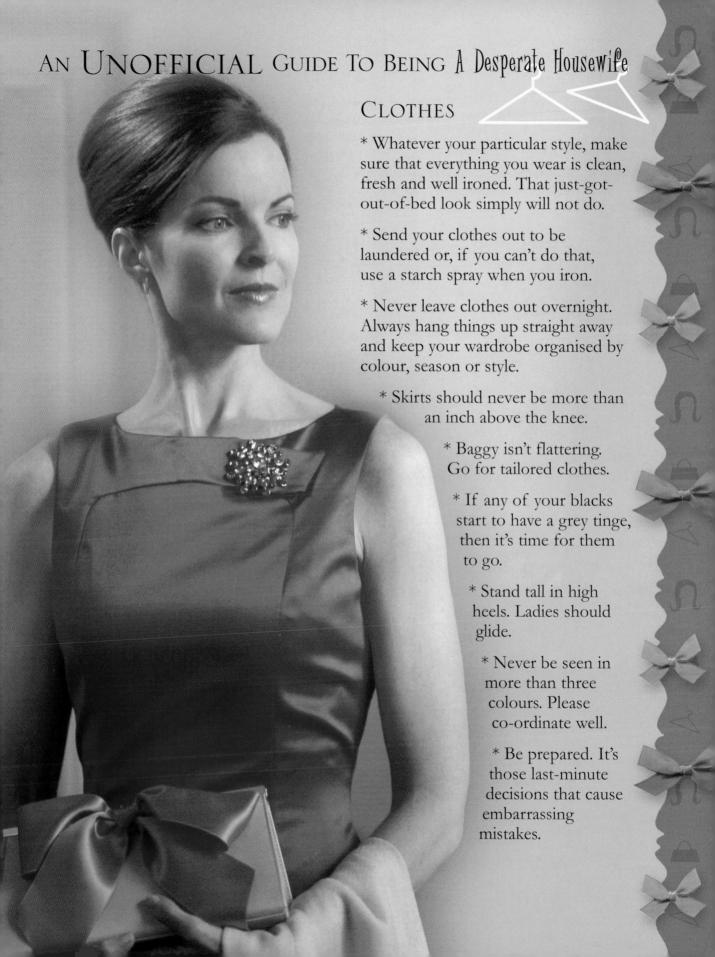

AN UNOFFICIAL GUIDE TO BEING A Desperate Housewife

CLOTHES

* Whatever your particular style, make sure that everything you wear is clean, fresh and well ironed. That just-got-out-of-bed look simply will not do.

* Send your clothes out to be laundered or, if you can't do that, use a starch spray when you iron.

* Never leave clothes out overnight. Always hang things up straight away and keep your wardrobe organised by colour, season or style.

* Skirts should never be more than an inch above the knee.

* Baggy isn't flattering. Go for tailored clothes.

* If any of your blacks start to have a grey tinge, then it's time for them to go.

* Stand tall in high heels. Ladies should glide.

* Never be seen in more than three colours. Please co-ordinate well.

* Be prepared. It's those last-minute decisions that cause embarrassing mistakes.

GET THE DESPERATE HOUSEWIFE LOOK

It doesn't matter how much they have going on in their lives, a desperate housewife always looks fabulous. And you should too. But don't stick to one look – mix and match for the perfect wardrobe.

LYNETTE
The Stressed-Out Mom

Practicality is key. Her wardrobe is inter-changeable, with blue and khaki as its staples. She mixes and matches jeans with vest tops and open shirts. Because she's always on the go, her shoes are flat – usually ballet pumps. Her accessories are plain – a simple silver necklace or neutral bangle.

BREE
The 50s Housewife

Bree is always immaculately turned out. Her classic look is usually made up of tweed, cashmere twinsets, and tailored shirts with slacks or on-the-knee pencil skirts. There is never a crease or stain. Her accessories are always simple and her pearls are usually the key feature.

SUSAN
The Girl Next Door

Susan's trousers are low-slung and tailored. They hug in all the right places, and teamed with tight, funky vests, look sexy without trying too hard. For the evening, Susan likes vibrant colours. If you have her dark colouring, try a red, fitted cardigan or a slim-fit purple kaftan with a hint of sequins. Most of her clothes could have come from her teenage daughter's wardrobe.

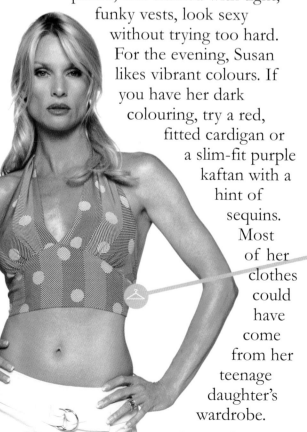

GABRIELLE
The Sexy Senorita

With her background in modelling, Gabrielle is the height of suburban chic. She loves tight-fitting denim and cropped halter-neck tops, or a micro mini and off-the-shoulder top. She bares lots of flesh to show off her olive skin. With her colouring she can carry off the brightest of colours and most daring prints. For the evening, only the most expensive haute couture will do. Day or night, she's dripping in diamonds and will never be seen without a pair of heels.

EDIE
The Tramp

The shorter and skimpier the better. She's another lover of skin-tight jeans and tiny spaghetti strap tops. For work she'll wear a little box jacket over a see-through blouse, and a short skirt. For relaxing or washing the car, she likes a pair of denim hotpants. For Edie, less is more.

GET THE DESPERATE HOUSEWIFE LOOK

Our models below show just how easy it is to look like a desperate housewife with clothes from your wardrobe. See our advice below.

THE MOTHER

Lynette's faded old jeans and tailored shirt are both comfortable and practical. Flat shoes are essential for child chasing. A large leather bag is a great accessory, and is perfect to carry around child-bribing toys and sweets.

LUNCH WITH THE GIRLS

Choose a skirt in a simple neutral tone such as black or white, and add strappy high heels to make your legs look longer. A silky camisole top always looks sexy. Add lots of bling at your throat and wrists. Take your designer (real or fake) handbag.

classic shirt

slinky camisole top

favourite jeans

tight skirt
for a sexy walk

flat shoes for
running after
children

high heels for extra leg length

An Unofficial Guide To Being A Desperate Housewife

Shopping

Elegance is key, even when paying a visit to your local mall. Go for a simple pleated skirt (below the knee of course) so you can get it on and off quickly in the changing rooms. Add a cardigan in a bright tone and a shopping basket. Don't forget your signature pearls.

Getting A Date

You'll need a dash of Susan and a hint of Edie. For day, try tailored jeans and a pretty shawl or cape, so you can give him a flash of shoulder and cleavage. For night, go for a tiny skirt and cute boots. You can't go wrong with a sexy pout under a cowboy hat. Your bag should only be big enough for your mobile, keys and lipstick.

cute cardie for warmth as dashing in and out of the shops

sexy hat to pout under

poncho/neurotic comfort blanket

skirt for getting on and off easily in the changing rooms

micro mini to flash lots of thigh

fitted jeans to show off your toned bottom

classic, yet comfy shoes

flip-flops to run around in

BREE'S GUIDE TO HOUSEHOLD MANAGEMENT

If you want your house to be show home perfect, then there's only one woman to turn to… Bree Van De Kamp.

1. There is no such thing as too much cleaning. Every day you should:
* vacuum the curtains
* clean the toilet
* wax wooden floors
* wipe the phone and computer keyboard with antiseptic wipes
* vacuum and plump up all cushions
* bleach every surface
* clean the oven and fridge.

2. Make sure that all the pictures in the house are perfectly level. Use a spirit level if necessary.

3. At the beginning of each week, prepare a list of dinner menus.

4. No watching TV until all homework and chores have been completed. No exceptions.

5. Check each day that any candles that have been used are discarded and replaced, and that all flowers are fresh.

6. There should be no such thing as 'best china'. All your china should be of an exceptionally high standard so you won't be embarrassed to use it when a neighbour pops round for tea. Speaking of which, always use a tea pot and tea leaves. Never, ever, brew tea from a bag in a cup.

7. Change the bedding on the spare bed once a week, even if it hasn't been slept in. This will ensure it always smells fresh and clean.

8. Bake every single day. Not only will the house smell simply delicious, but there will always be lovely treats available for visitors and the children. Baskets of cupcakes are always popular.

9. Give the children's bedrooms a routine inspection every week. Don't tell them when this will be to ensure they always keep it clean. N.B. This is also a perfect opportunity to check for any contraband items.

10. Ask guests to take off their shoes in the hall. I'm sure they're aware of how many germs we all carry around. If anyone has bad feet or no socks, have a handy supply of paper slippers on standby.

THE PERFECT DESPERATE DINNER PARTY

A Wisteria Lane dinner party isn't any ordinary affair.
With the eclectic mix of all the residents, there's always
amazing food, scintillating conversation and enough gossip
to ensure the evening is talked about for months.
Here's how to host your very own desperate dinner party.

ORGANISE

If you have someone
like Bree on your street
you know that any party
will be planned with
military precision. Make
sure you're involved from
the beginning as you don't
want her taking over
completely.

Decide on a venue – any house
but yours is good.

Invitations – you will want to
keep the numbers down so
as to give the evening
exclusivity. And don't invite
the person you want to
talk about.

Assign tasks – who will
be in charge of
food, wine,
decoration etc?

FOOD

Everybody brings a dish. The house
owner co-ordinates so you don't
get twelve desserts and no
vegetables. Or you could always
do a Gabrielle – order it in
and pass it off as home-
cooking. Just don't do a
Susan and burn
everything.

DECORATE

Table decoration is very important. You will need a stunning floral centrepiece and elegant candles for the perfect lighting.

Make sure you have enough crockery and cutlery before the night – the Bree in your life will not accept mismatched place settings.

The tricky part is the seating arrangement. When Susan had everyone over for lunch, Edie made a lunge for the seat next to Mike while Susan was taking coats. Then Bree ended up far too close to the kitchen, so she saw Susan take the muffins out of the packet rather than out of the oven. It's vital that you get it right.

MUSIC AND WINE

With so many different people, it's impossible to please everyone. Gabrielle types like to unwind with something latino, while someone like Edie responds to something hard and loud. So the best idea is usually some inoffensive easy listening background music from the latest chart wonder.

Regarding wine, you want enough to feel like flirting with other people's husbands, but not so much that you actually try and take them home.

DESPERATE DINNER PARTY ADVICE

The women of Wisteria Lane all have very different ideas about what makes a good party. Here are some tips on doing it their way.

BREE

* Perfection takes planning, so never leave anything until the last minute. Menus should be written out a week in advance and you should have a checklist to refer to daily to make sure you've covered every detail.

* The table should look like a page from *Good Housekeeping* magazine. It's a good idea to have a folder of ideas for centrepieces and place settings, so you can choose a theme and then spend at least two days making some special designs.

* When laying the table, it's important that everything is perfect. Use a ruler to align cutlery and make sure that the wine glasses are in exactly the same position all around the table.

SUSAN

* If you're not the best cook in the world, then why not arrange a Pot Luck evening where everybody brings a dish. At least that way you know that something will be edible.

* Get your daughter to help with the cooking and place settings.

* If one of the women in the road is after your man, then for goodness sake don't invite them!

GABRIELLE

* Get the maid to arrange and lay the table.

* Order the food in from the most expensive restaurant in town and then hide the cartons it came in.

* Spend at least two hours getting ready – after all, you never know who might turn up.

LYNETTE

* If you've completely forgotten about it until the day of the party, palm your kids off on one of the neighbours and get cooking. There must be something in the freezer that can be turned into three courses.

* If you can't get a babysitter, bribe the kids into submission. Rent them their ten favourite DVDs, set them up in the den and fill the room with all the treats they are never usually allowed to have, as long as they promise not to make too much noise and only to leave the room for quick toilet breaks.

* Get drunk.

EDIE

* Buy yourself a really sexy new outfit.

* Don't waste time cooking – order a chinese take-out.

* Make sure there's at least two men to every woman – you don't want to go hungry now, do you?

STRAWBERRY AND CHAMPAGNE SOUP

(S e r v e s   6)

Although very seductive sipped from large wine glasses, it can also be served in glass bowls, with spoons, if you are feeling a little more reserved.

375g (12oz) strawberries

150g (5oz) caster sugar

250ml (12floz) freshly squeezed orange juice

3 flutes of Champagne or sparkling dry white wine

Purée the strawberries (reserving a few for garnish) with the sugar and the orange juice. Divide the mixture between six dishes or large wine glasses. Top up with chilled champagne and garnish.

MEXICAN LIVING

All the residents of Wisteria Lane have tastefully decorated houses, but the most striking décor on the street has to be that of Carlos and Gabrielle Solis. So let's see how you too can get that hacienda-style.

The basic decoration of the house has a neutral tone. The walls are a variation of either taupe or white. Try painting your walls with warm, but neutral shades, then adding colour in striking pictures or luxurious curtains. If you can't afford the prices charged by fashionable artists, try visiting second-hand bookshops, as they often have stunning prints. Or you could try flea markets to pick up a bargain.

THE LOUNGE

Gabrielle's lounge has a slight feel of a cathedral, with large, heavy sofas and dark wood tables and ornaments, plus the exceedingly large candlesticks on either side of the fireplace. You can pick up dark oak at almost any second-hand furniture shop and if you can find a beautiful table or sofa, make a feature of it and buy ornaments to match.

The Bedroom

This should be your piéce de résistance as it's your retreat from the world. Get the largest bed you can afford and let it dominate the centre, preferable with a heavy wooden base. Pile on richly coloured cushions from any store. A large wardrobe is a must, so spend time trawling around second-hand shops or auctions to get one the same tone of wood as the bed. Finally, add silk lanterns and hangings to match your curtains and if you have company, light candles around the room for a seductive glow.

Furnishings

Large candles on tall, ornamental candlesticks will give a lovely feeling of warmth and intimacy when you have friends round. If you can afford a real wood floor, then do. Not only does it look and feel gorgeous, but it increases your property's saleability. Finally, invest in a beautiful Mexican rug that enhances the colours you've put in your room. You can pick up some wonderful bargains from *eBay*.

WORKING WITH THE HIRED HELP

When you have got as much going on in your life as the residents of Wisteria Lane, you may need to employ staff to ease the load. Here's how to deal with them the desperate housewife way.

THE GARDENER

If you're going to be looking at someone wandering round your garden half naked all summer, then it just makes sense to ensure that they're easy on the eye.

If you choose a young gardener, then not only will you have to pay them less than a more experienced one, but they'll also be more accommodating when it comes to doing odd jobs around the house.

Gardeners are a great choice to have an affair with – just ask Gabrielle. They've got a winning touch and if your bushes are big enough they can be at your house an awful lot so their visits won't arouse suspicion.

Top Tip: If he's a good gardener, don't let him get too attached to you. If he does you'll have to get rid of him to finish the affair, and your grass will suffer.

AN UNOFFICIAL GUIDE TO BEING A Desperate Housewife

THE POOL MAN

It's a well-known fact that pool men are the easiest types of men to have affairs with. They are renowned for their sexy six-packs and long, long hoses. So, if you're feeling the need to indulge in some light extra-curricular activity, then get a pool man immediately.

Top Tip: If you haven't got a swimming pool, be nice to your husband and demand he builds you one as soon as possible. Tell him you think you're getting fat and it's putting you off sex. That should do it.

THE MAID

You have to be careful when picking a maid, because she will end up knowing everything about you. She needs to be trustworthy and, if at all possible, open to blackmail.

A non-English-speaking maid is a good choice because she can't understand everything that's going on, but this can cause problems with obeying your instructions.

She should be willing to take on various duties, such as cooking, cleaning and shopping, and anything else that's too tiring for you to do.

Top Tip: If you nearly get caught out by your husband when your lover leaves a sock in the bedroom, get her to cover for you by using a sock to polish the furniture.

Keeping The Neighbourhood Watch

(By Martha Huber)

These days you're not safe in your own home, so it's important that neighbours look out for each other. With a neighbour like Martha Huber, someone's always watching – whether you want them to or not. Here's Martha's guide to keeping the Neighbourhood Watch.

1. It's important to know everyone in the street. If anyone new moves in, make sure you're the first to welcome them. Why not take them round a nice casserole as a little 'welcome to the lane' gift?

2. Keep up-to-date on the local gossip. That way you'll know exactly who should and shouldn't be coming and going, day or night. It's not that you're nosy – it just makes good sense to know what's going on in your road.

3. Make contact with the local Chief of Police. Then if you're worried about any strange goings-on you can give him a call to express your concerns and you won't have to worry about him not taking your call. After all, you have made it your job to befriend his wife.

4. Drop in on your neighbours on a regular basis. Don't wait to be asked – you'll be surprised how many people forget. Just wait until you know they're home and knock on the door. This is a great way to find out all the latest news and keep communication flowing.

5. Keep your windows clean. It's important to get a clear view into everyone's house and sometimes binoculars really struggle to focus through grime.

6. Know everyone's schedule. For example, what time the husbands go to work or the wives go shopping, or even what time the gardener turns up.

7. If you suspect anybody is up to no good – seeing other men behind their husband's back or trying to dispose of dead bodies – then it's best to have it out with them as soon as possible. Don't let things fester.

8. If you spot something suspicious happening in a house – for example, you hear a gunshot – then a good way to get a closer look is to return an item you may have borrowed some time ago. A blender would work well in this scenario.

9. You should keep your own secrets and past to yourself. This is purely so other people's judgement isn't clouded by tittle tattle about you. You should try to remain impartial and slightly aloof – you are head of the Neigbourhood Watch after all.

10. Always befriend the most unpopular person in the street as they are usually the most eager to divulge useful information about the other residents. It doesn't really matter if you like that person or not, what really matters is that they can find out details that you aren't privy to.

N.B. It's a good idea not to get murdered.

KEEPING THE HEDGES TRIMMED

To John, gardening is more than just pushing a lawnmower around. He loves his job — and the perks it provides. So here are a few of his top tips on maintaining a perfect garden…

PLANNING

The ladies of Wisteria Lane are very particular about their gardens so you need a well-thought-out design that makes the best use of your space. Mrs Solis wants lots of beautiful vistas that all her neighbours can see and admire, as well as some shady nooks and secret corners that the neighbours can't see at all.

THE LAWN

A well-kept lawn is the centrepiece of a fine garden. It should be mown and watered regularly. Mr Solis likes me to spray his lawns at least twice a day, even when there's a water restriction in hot weather. He says it's important I should keep everything moist and I do my best.

Trees and Shrubs

Trees, shrubs and hedges are an essential feature of gardens and they don't need much work, apart from pruning and trimming. I take care to keep our shrubs well-cut and sometimes I trim them into shapes. When Edie Brit saw my cones and balls she said she would like me to do something exciting with *her* shrubs, but Mrs Solis told her I was too busy and anyway there are families with young children in Wisteria Lane.

Climbing Plants

Climbers are very versatile and can be grown on all kinds of structures. A flowering climbing plant looks really great against an old wall. Mrs Solis loves plants so much she asked me to put a strong climber right under her bedroom window.

Flowers

Sowing annuals from seed is the cheapest and easiest way of making a colourful display in your garden. Mr Solis likes to give Mrs Solis a bunch of fresh flowers every day so he tells me to plant my seeds as often as I want. Mrs Solis agrees. I do like to keep my employers happy.

LETTERS PAGE

Your favourite housewives answer your problems.

Dear Bree

My husband has started getting a bit kinky in bed. It was only little things at first, like spanking him with my hairbrush, but now he wants me to dress up as a Star Wars Storm Trooper and use a strap-on. Should I do it?

Sarah, Stoke-on-Trent

Oh my goodness! You need to put a stop to this right now. If you give in to his depraved demands, things will only get worse. Before you know it you'll be strapped naked to the basement ceiling having all manner of hot objects poked into you. The next time he brings this up – slap him across the face. If he continues in these disgusting fantasies, march him to the nearest psychiatrist's office.

Dear Edie

I'm 25 and still a virgin. I want to wait until I meet Mr Right, but all my friends are having sex and I'm feeling a bit left out. Do you think I should wait?

Diana, Dorset

You're kidding! 25 and still a virgin – surely that's not healthy? Let's be brutally honest, if you're waiting for Mr Right, you're going to be waiting for an awfully long time because there's no such thing. Men are arrogant pigs who only want one thing. So take what you want – chew 'em up and spit 'em out. Get laid – you don't know what you're missing.

Dear Lynette

I've got a three-year-old and a five-year-old. While I've loved being at home with them, I'm thinking about going back to work. Do you think I should?

Heather, Grimsby

YES. Don't hesitate for a moment, just grab your briefcase and run straight back into employment as fast as your exhausted legs can carry you. You could soon be back in the land of the living and having conversations with grown-ups. Oh, the joy of not being covered in food and vomit, of wearing a nice Prada suit and going out for long, boozy lunches.

Dear Susan

I have the biggest crush on my gym instructor, and I'm too shy to tell him in case he laughs at me. He is drop dead gorgeous and I'm sure he could have his pick of the girls. Should I risk the embarrassment of being turned down and tell him anyway?

Liz, South Wales

Oh it's horrible when you get a crush on someone – you'd think you'd grow out of it, but you never do! Honestly though, you should go for it, what have you got to lose? Get him to show you the correct way to do a lateral pull-down and then gently lean back into him. If he doesn't respond, then you know he's not interested. Or gay! And you can always change gyms.

Dear Gabrielle

I'm 35 and I'm having improper thoughts about my son's 17-year-old friend. The worst thing is, I think he likes me too. What should I do?

Alison, Leicester

Go for it girl! Life's too short to worry about doing the right thing. Besides, it's legal and it's not hurting anybody, so why not?! Although perhaps it's for the best if you don't tell too many people about it.

Dear Mrs Huber

I pride myself on knowing what's happening in my street and recently I've become suspicious about the woman at No. 20. There are strange people coming and going all times of the day and night, and lots of noise coming from the upstairs bedrooms. What should I do?

Ellie, East London

Firstly, well done on your vigilance. With people like you, the world is a safer place. Have you got a friendly policeman you can call to complain to and ask to investigate? If not, get some neighbours on board and go round and confront her. By the sound of things, she's definitely up to no good.

WHICH DESPERATE HOUSEWIFE ARE YOU?

1. You and your friend both fancy the same man, but he asks you out. Do you…

a) Feel so bad about upsetting your friend that you tell him you can't make it.

b) Feel guilty about going behind her back, but rush straight out for a bikini wax.

c) Tell him that you would never betray a friendship and he should be ashamed of himself.

d) Get all excited, but forget to keep it a secret from your friend who falls out with you.

e) Pop round to your friend's house to ask her if the outfit you've chosen is sexy enough.

2. Your interfering mother-in-law is coming to stay and you're not very happy. Do you…

a) Grin and bear it while muttering obscenities under your breath.

b) Pretend you're overjoyed, while secretly planning visits to your lover.

c) Write a checklist for her visit to remember to change the bedding and put fresh flowers in her room.

d) Forget about it completely until she turns up on your doorstep.

e) Stay with friends until she leaves.

3. You've heard that a neighbour's husband is having an affair. Do you…

a) Drop hints hoping that she'll work it out.

b) Tell her, but get her to look on the positive side. She'll now be able to get some extra curricular action without feeling guilty.

c) March round to his office and tell him that he either stops seeing other women or you'll tell his wife.

d) Invite her for coffee and tell her the latest gossip about one of the neighbour's cheating before realising that it's her you're talking about.

e) Give him a call to see when he's next available for a 'working' lunch.

4. A friend has just had a horrible haircut and asks your opinion. Do you…

a) Mumble some unintelligible comments about hair in general and quickly change the subject.

b) Tell her that headscarves are making a comeback and offer to buy her a few.

c) Suggest that a few highlights would make it look even better.

d) Tell you that you hadn't even noticed she'd had it cut and what did it look like before?

e) Laugh and tell her that she looks like a butch version of Dale Winton.

5. You're on a first date with a gorgeous new man and he asks you to suck his toes. Do you…

a) Feel obliged, gingerly take off his socks and use the very tip of your tongue.

b) Say that's fine by you, as long as he'll do you some sexual favours in return.

c) Resign yourself and go to the kitchen for some spray disinfectant before you get started.

d) Tell him you've got far better things to be doing and promptly unzip his trousers.

e) Fall to your knees, pop his whole foot in your mouth and put it through a spin cycle.

6. The PTA are putting on a children's show and you're making the costumes. You're rubbish at sewing. Do you…

a) Panic and ask the neighbourhood ladies to help you out.

b) Get your maid to do it.

c) Buy a book on sewing and study it so you can make the best costumes the PTA have ever seen.

d) Just do it, not worrying that the trees have no branches and the sheep only have two legs.

e) Sleep with the man at the local fancy dress shop and get costumes for free.

Mostly a's
You're just like Susan Mayer. You're sweet and sensitive and a bit of a klutz, but that's why everybody loves you. You're desperate for love, but you won't go to any lengths to get it if it means hurting someone you care about. You are destined for true happiness one day.

Mostly b's
What a sexy temptress you are – just like Gabrielle Solis. You're comfortable in your own skin and while you love your female friends, you love men even more. You're never happier than when a man desires you and fortunately, you will always have men falling at your feet.

Mostly c's
Goodness me, Miss Prissy-knickers, lighten up! Just like Bree Van De Kamp, you control every situation and can't stand chaos or disorder. But you do have good points…

You're kind and caring and would do anything for your friends and family. But chill out a bit, or you could find yourself alone in old age!

Mostly d's
Just like Lynette Scavo you're exhausting to be around. Your friends adore you, even though you can be too straight-talking at times and hurt their feelings, but they know you don't mean it. Try to take some time out for yourself though or your nerves could get frayed.

Mostly e's
There's no beating around the bush – you're a tramp. Just like Edie Britt, men are your life and you want them all to fancy you. But be careful – beauty doesn't last forever, one day you're going to have to show that there's more to you or you could be left on the shelf forever.

WHICH DESPERATE HUSBAND IS YOUR PARTNER?

1. A new neighbour moves in – she's young, sexy, blonde and has enormous boobs. Would he…

a) Suggest you go round and introduce yourself – it's only neighbourly after all.

b) Be friendly, but not really make an effort to get to know her.

c) Imagine her in a leather catsuit.

d) Not even notice she'd moved in.

e) Suddenly start jogging past her house in tight shorts every morning.

2. There's a rumour that the police are staking out someone in your street. Would he…

a) Dismiss it as a silly mix-up.

b) Get his buddies in the force to do a little investigation into what they're doing.

c) Be on his best behaviour and not put himself in any compromising positions for a while.

d) Pack up his family and leave town.

e) Destroy any incriminating evidence he may have lying around the house – just in case.

3. You have an emergency dentist appointment, so you call him at work to ask him to pick up the kids. Would he…

a) Be a bit grumpy about having to leave the office, but enjoy it once he got there.

b) Get there early and take them for ice-cream.

c) Not get the message as he was busy.

d) Not mind going, but refuse to get out of the car and talk to the other parents.

e) Get one of his henchmen to collect them.

4. You tell your partner that the other girls in the street have suggested a swinger's party. Would he…

a) Laugh and say that he'd be up for it, but not take it seriously.

b) Tell you you're all the woman he needs and chase you upstairs to prove it.

c) Use all his powers of persuasion to try to talk you into it.

d) Tell you not to be so ridiculous even talking about such things.

e) Quite like the idea as long as it's only him doing the swinging.

5. The local busybody is trying to set up a neighbourhood watch scheme. Would he…

a) Think it's a brilliant idea.

b) Suggest that it would be great for you to get involved, but he'd rather keep out of it.

c) Be well up for it if he can watch the neighbours through his binoculars.

d) Say that people are far too nosy and interfering as it is and to keep out of it.

e) Tell you to sign up immediately – anything to keep you busy at night.

6. You've bought a new Liz Hurley-style revealing dress. Would he…

a) Tell you you look beautiful but that it might be too much for dinner with his firm's elderly partners.

b) Convince you to wear it when you get cold feet as you look gorgeous in it.

c) Take you straight upstairs for a good seeing-to while still wearing it.

d) Call you a slut and demand you take it off.

e) Tell you how sexy you look, but you'd better wear a cardie as he doesn't want other men drooling over you.

Mostly a's

You've got a good one here, just like Tom Scavo. While he may not set the world on fire, there's nothing like a bit of protection and security to make you feel safe and loved. You'll always be happy and he'll always look after you – just make sure you remind him to bring a little excitement into the relationship every now and again.

Mostly b's

He's as cool and sexy as Mike Delfino. Even though he doesn't want to give too much away about his life and his past, he will be open and honest when it comes to you. He'll always be faithful and true to you and will keep you safe. A relationship most of us would kill for, filled with passion and romance. Lucky you!

Mostly c's

You need to watch this one. Just like Rex Van De Kamp, he may seem like Mr Average on the surface, but there's a whole other side buried beneath the Pringle jumpers. So if you're in for the long haul with him, then get digging. It's best to get all that dirty laundry out in the open as soon as possible. You don't want any surprises ten years down the line.

Mostly d's

Like Paul Young, there are secrets and lies buried here – and we're not talking little white ones. He may seem perfectly sane and reasonable, if not a little straight-laced, but don't trust him. What you see is not always what you get, and you could be heading for a whole heap of trouble if you decide to stay with him. Be wary.

Mostly e's

He has the fire of Carlos Solis, which can be incredibly exciting, but incredibly dangerous too. He will worship and adore you, but while it's great to be loved, it's not so great to be smothered. Tell him he has to give you some space to breathe. You can't be at his beck and call all the time.

ACKNOWLEDGMENTS

The publishers would like to thank the following for their kind permission to reproduce their photographs:

r= right; l= left; a= above; b= below; c= centre; t= top.

Back jacket: Getty Images/ Photodisc Collection. Page 4-5: Corbis/ David Papazion. Page 6: Getty Images/ Steve Taylor. Page 7: Getty Images/ Stuart O'Sullivan. Page 8bl: Corbis/ Matthias Kulka. Page 9: Rex Features. Page 10-11: Rex Features. Page 12: Rex Features. Page 16: Big Pictures. Page 17bc: Rex Features. Page 17br: Getty Images/ James Baigrie. Page 18: Big Pictures. Page 20-21: Big Pictures. Page 22: Alamy/ ap-images. Page 23: Alamy/ Carlos Davila. Page 24: Rex Features. Page 25: Big Pictures. Page 26: Corbis/ Thom Lang. Page 27: Katz/ Gamma. Page 28: Rex Features. Page 29: Getty Images/ Julie Toy. Page 30: Alamy/ Dynamics Graphics Group/ Creatas.

Page 31: Rex Features. Page 32-33: Corbis/ Matthias Kulka. Page 33: Rex Features. Page 34: Big Pictures. Page 35c: Getty Images/ Davies & Starr. Page 37: Rex Features. Page 39: Katz/ Gamma. Page 40: Big Pictures. Page 41: Big Pictures. Page 45: Katz/ Gamma. Page 46: Rex Features. Page 46-47: Corbis/ Voker Mohrke. Page 48b: Corbis/ H. Armstrong Roberts. Page 48-49: Alamy/ Foodfolio. Page 50: Katz/ Gamma. Page 51: Katz/ Gamma. Page 52: Katz/ Gamma. Page 53: Rex Features. Page 54-55: Alamy/ Suzy Bennett. Page 55: Getty Images/ Stephen Shugerman. Page 56: Big Pictures. Page 57: Alamy/ Mark Wood. Page 59r: Big Pictures. Page 59bl: Getty Images/ Photodisc Collection. Page 60: Big Pictures. 61c: Katz/ Gamma. Page 61tr: Corbis/ Thom Lang. Page 62bl: Katz/ Gamma. Page 62c: Rex Features. Page 62r: Rex Features. Page 63: Rex Features.